START-A-CRAFT

Tie-Dyeing

Get started in a new craft with easy-to-follow

projects for beginners

C ELIA B UCHANAN

CHARTWELL
BOOKS, INC.

A QUINTET BOOK

Published by Chartwell Books
A Division of Book Sales, Inc.
114 Northfield Avenue
Edison, New Jersey 08837

ISBN 0-7858-1002-1

This book was designed and produced by
Quintet Publishing Limited
6 Blundell Street
London N7 9BH

Creative Director: Richard Dewing
Designer: James Lawrence
Project Editor: Anna Briffa
Editor: Lydia Darbyshire
Photographer: Nick Bailey

Typeset in Great Britain by
Central Southern Typesetters, Eastbourne
Manufactured in Singapore by Eray Scan Pte Ltd
Printed in China by Leefung-Asco Printers Trading Ltd

ACKNOWLEDGEMENTS

Quintet Publishing plc would like to thank
George Weil & Sons and Sinotex
for providing the art materials and fabrics for making the projects
photographed in this book. Addresses to contact are:

The Warehouse	George Weil & Sons
Reading Arch Road	18 Hanson Street
Redhill, Surrey	London
RH1 1HG	W1P 7DB
England	England

The author would like to offer thanks to Celia Papadopoulos for her
assistance in assembling the projects in the book.

CONTENTS

INTRODUCTION

———◆———

Tie-dyeing, one of the oldest and one of the simplest methods of producing patterned fabric, is considered to be a "resist" method of dyeing, similar to batik. Many types of pattern can be achieved by binding or folding the fabric, then immersing it in a dye bath. Complex-looking, multicolored patterns can be made by refolding and rebinding the fabric each time a new color is added, and modern cold water dyes allow spectacular effects to be obtained easily and safely. You will find most of the materials you need in your home, so you will not need to buy expensive equipment before you can get started.

Early evidence that tie-dyeing was widely used to produce patterned fabrics can be found in the *sima* charters from Indonesia, which mention tie-dyers as one of the five different kinds of textile worker producing fabric in the early 10th century. It is likely, however, that tie-dyeing was used as a method of patterning fabric in that region even before that date. One of the earliest techniques of tie-dyeing to be used was *ikat* – a method of tying resist material around yarn and dyeing before weaving – which added subtle variations of color to simple geometric designs. *Ikat* was also extensively used in Africa, and some of the most elaborate uses of the technique can be found among the people of western Madagascar.

Pelangi, the technique most often associated with tie-dyeing, produces the familiar circular and striped patterns that can be found on many modern tie-dyed fabrics. Traditionally, fabric decorated with circular patterns was hung on poles outside the houses of dead people, and these sacred textiles, known as *poritutu coto*, were produced by the people of the Rongkong region of the island of Sulawesi in eastern Indonesia. Similarly, in Morocco Berber women made head scarves with rectangular or mirror patterns, which were used to ward off the evil eye.

One of the more complicated methods of tie-dyeing is *teritik,* which involves stitching areas of the fabric to resist the dye. Some of the earliest evidence of the trade in this type of tie-dyed fabric was found in a list of fabrics exported from Indonesia in 1580. The Indonesian word *teritik* means "to drip consecutively in little drops," and this phrase accurately describes the effect that can be achieved by the technique. The use of stitching in *teritik* means that, unlike in *pelangi*, a more controlled, sometimes even pictorial pattern can be achieved.

In the West the technique became fashionable in the 1960s and 1970s, often resulting in some rather garish designs. More recently, however, western designers have been adapting the traditional methods of *pelangi* and *teritik* to produce elaborate and subtly colored patterns. Spectacular results can be produced by over-dyeing, and rainbow-colored designs are easily achievable.

Pinching, folding and binding or sewing the fabrics prevents the dye from reaching those areas of the material that are covered by the resist material, and those parts that are not exposed to the dye remain uncolored. The end result is determined by the way in which the fabric is folded, bound and stitched before dyeing, and subsequent re-folding and dyeing enables a variety of patterns and colors to be built up.

As with other forms of surface patterning or dyeing, the best results are usually obtained when the fabric is decorated before it is made up into the garment. However, if simple garments are selected, it is possible to overcome the problems that are caused by seams so that even those with only limited sewing abilities can produce some really eye-catching patterns.

Even in its simplest forms tie-dyeing offers a way of achieving a wide variety of patterns, and vibrant or subtle colors can be used to give different effects. Combining these simple, ancient processes with modern materials allows an enormous range of personal and individual patterns to be produced by this versatile craft.

EQUIPMENT AND MATERIALS

The projects in this book have been designed to demonstrate a variety of tie-dyeing techniques, and each project takes you through the steps involved in creating the finished items. The materials and techniques required for each project are described in detail, and as you work through the projects you will build up your own "library" of dyeing techniques. Slightly more complex methods and articles are introduced in the later projects, and newcomers to the craft can work through the early pieces to develop their confidence and expertise so that they will be able to design and create their own items, and experimenting with different materials and techniques will show just what a versatile and enjoyable craft this is.

You will find most of the equipment you will need in your home. Several different kinds of fabric dye are available, although those most suitable for tie-dyeing are the cold water dyes. (Before you begin make sure that the dye you intend to use is suitable for the fabric with which you will be working.) In general, it is easier to dye 100 per cent natural fibers – silk, cotton, wool and linen, for example, or a combination of these. Synthetic fabrics or mixes of natural and synthetic fibers do not dye evenly, and you will have to use special dyes for these fabrics.

You will need

◇ Old newspaper or a plastic sheet to protect your work surface
◇ Scissors and a craft knife
◇ As wide a variety of winding materials as possible – string, thread, wool, twine, strips of fabric (from old sheets etc) and elastic bands
◇ 30 wooden or plastic clothes pegs (those with metal springs are best)
◇ 50 paper clips in various sizes
◇ Glass marbles or balls or stones (about 30 small, 10 medium sized and 4 large)

◇ 5 corks in various sizes
◇ Old buttons in various sizes
◇ Rubber gloves (the thin, surgical ones are best)
◇ Plastic bucket or large plastic bowl
◇ Electric kettle or saucepan and hot plate
◇ 1 teaspoon
◇ 1 tablespoon
◇ Large, heat-proof measuring jug that holds 2 pints
◇ 1lb table salt
◇ 1 pint vinegar

You will also need some cold water dyes. When you select your dyes weigh the fabric and check the quantity of dye you need for each item or items. Each manufacturer gives specific recipes and instructions for its own products, so although general instructions of mixing cold water dyes are given in the instructions for each project, you must always check the manufacturer's instructions for the dye you are using. The quantities given in these mixing instructions will dye approximately 64 x 64 inches of fabric.

You will also, of course, need materials and garments, as well as a few accessories, and these are listed for each product.

MIXING DYES FOR COTTON

1 Mix each dye, remembering to check the manufacturer's instructions for the dye that you are using. Approximately you will need to add 1 teaspoon of dye to each pint of boiling water in a heat-proof jug.

2 Add 2 tablespoons of salt and mix thoroughly.

3 Add this solution to a bowl containing 4 pints of hot water and stir.

4 You can check the strength of the dye by placing a strip of the fabric you are using in the dye bath for 10–15 minutes. If the color is too strong, add more boiling water; if it is too weak, add more dye.

MIXING DYES FOR SILK AND WOOL

1 Add 1 teaspoon of dye to each pint of boiling water in a heat-proof jug.

2 Add 2 tablespoons of vinegar and mix thoroughly. Add this to a further 2 pints of hot water and stir.

TYING METHODS AND EXAMPLES

There are numerous ways of tying fabric to achieve patterns, and each one will produce a different end result. Even if you tie several pieces of material in the same way, you will not be able to produce exactly the same pattern each time, and this is one of the exciting things about tie-dyeing – you never know exactly how a piece will turn out, and every one is individual and personal.

MARBLED PATTERN

Crumple the fabric into a hard ball and bind it with twine or string. For each different color, rc-crumple the fabric in a different way. When you are dyeing larger pieces of material, bunch the fabric along its length and bind it into a sausage-like shape. You can add greater definition to the pattern by brushing fabric paint onto the fabric after it is dry but before untying it.

CHECK PATTERN

Evenly pleat the fabric and iron it, then secure the pleats with clothes pegs.

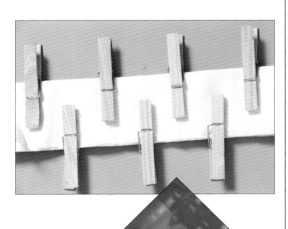

STRIPES

Fold the fabric in half, pleat it and bind it in the centre with string.

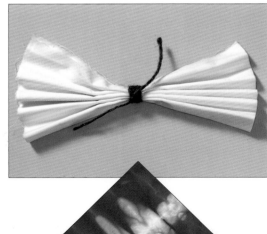

SMALL CIRCLES

Tie small round objects – marbles or stones – intc the fabric.

VIGNETTE EFFECTS

Roll the fabric tightly around a cord then ruche it. Repeat the process by wrapping the fabric in opposite directions and re-dyeing it with a different color.

FRAGMENTED PATTERN

Pinch the center of the fabric and allow it to fall into drapes like a closed umbrella. Cross-bind it with thread or twine.

RIBS

Make neat folds and secure the pleats at regular intervals with paper clips.

VARIABLE STRIPES

Fold the fabric in half, pleat it and bind it at intervals with twine or thread.

ELABORATE CIRCLES

Wrap a champagne cork into the fabric and tie it with thin twine or thread.

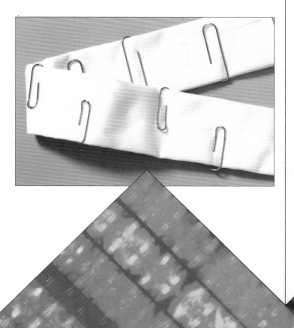

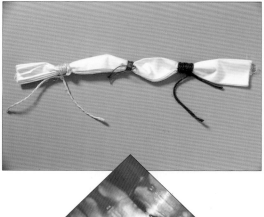

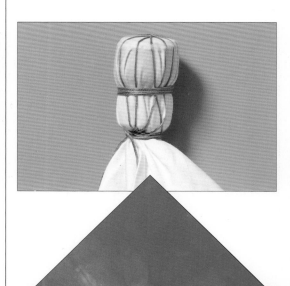

ASYMMETRIC PATTERN

Knot each corner with a piece of fabric from the center of a square of material. This technique is best done with lightweight fabrics.

BOLD STRIPES

Simply knot the fabric at intervals.

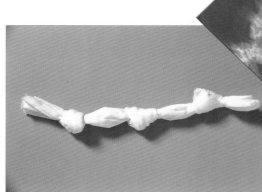

CONCENTRIC PATTERN

Pinch the center of the fabric and allow it to fall into drapes like a closed umbrella. Bind it at intervals lengthways.

SQUARES

Take a square of fabric and fold it diagonally twice so that it makes a triangle. Pleat the fabric lengthways and bind it with thread.

FRACTURED GLASS PATTERN

Fold the fabric once or twice, then twist and allow it to twist back on itself before binding it with twine.

TABLE NAPKINS

◆

This first project uses a square patterning method and a single color to make some table napkins. The materials listed below – except the dye itself – are sufficient for one napkin, so if you want to make more, you will need to multiply the quantities accordingly. You can, if you prefer, use ready-made napkins. Remember to use pure natural fibers.

You will need
- ◇ 1 square of cotton, 8 x 8 inches
- ◇ Electric iron
- ◇ Clothes pegs (optional)
- ◇ 36 inches string
- ◇ ½ teaspoon cornflower blue cold water dye (sufficient for 6 napkins)
- ◇ 2 tablespoons salt
- ◇ Heat-proof jug large enough to hold 2 pints
- ◇ 1 bowl, large enough to hold 6 pints
- ◇ Rubber gloves

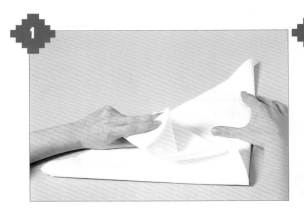

1 Iron the fabric to remove unwanted creases and folds. This will both make it easier to fold the cloth as you want and help to prevent the dye from adhering to areas of the cloth you do not want to be colored. Fold the square over on itself diagonally to form a triangle then fold it again to make a smaller triangle. To ensure that the pattern was soft, we did not iron these folds in.

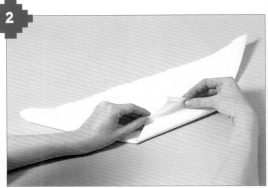

2 Place the folded square in front of you with the apex of the triangle towards you and fold the top over by 1 inch. Using that as a guide, continue to fold down the material to form a long strip.

3 You may want to hold the pleats with clothes pegs to stop them from unfolding while you work.

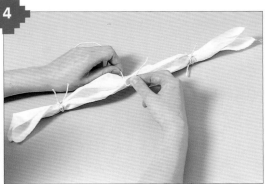

4 Each napkin will require five pieces of string, each about 7 inches long. Bind the first piece of string several times around the center of the strip and tie it tightly.

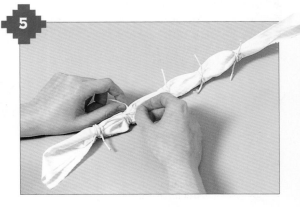

5 Repeat this at the ends, then tie pieces about half-way along each end or where the folds are beginning to open.

6 Mix ⅛ teaspoon of blue dye to 1 pint of boiling water in a heat-proof jug. Add 2 tablespoons of salt and mix thoroughly. Place the bound square in the dye bath for 10–15 minutes – but check the manufacturer's instructions – and stir occasionally to make sure that the dye is even.

7 Once the fabric is the color you want, remove the bundle or bundles from the bowl and rinse thoroughly under cold running water. When the water runs clear, most of the excess dye will have washed out. Untie the string.

8 When the fabric is completely dry, iron it and hem or overstitch the edges.

TIP

• Some dye manufacturers produce an after-treatment for their products, which prevents too much color washing out, and you may want to consider using one of these if the items you make are likely to require frequent washing.

CARDS AND JEWELRY

◆

Now that you have tried one of the basic methods, you can combine several techniques, including over-dyeing, to produce more intricate, multicolored patterns. Mastering the basic binding and dyeing techniques will make it easier for you to visualize the likely end results, and making personalized gift tags, greetings cards and jewelry from these samples is an ideal way of using your early experimental pieces.

You will need

◇ 2 pieces of habutai silk, finely woven, each 12 x 12 inches
◇ 15 feet heavy thread or embroidery thread
◇ ½ teaspoon each of red, yellow and blue dye
◇ 3 tablespoons vinegar (but check manufacturer's instructions)
◇ 6 feet twine
◇ 5 small marbles or glass balls
◇ 2–3 bowls, each large enough to hold 1 pint
◇ Electric iron
◇ 1 sheet of A1 (33⅛ x 23⅜ inches) card or ready-made greetings card and gift card blanks
◇ 1 pair of earring findings or blanks of your choice
◇ 2 brooch findings
◇ 4 blank button covers, ¼ inch across
◇ Scissors and a craft knife
◇ Clear, all-purpose adhesive

1 Take one piece of silk, scrunch it into a tight ball and bind it with embroidery thread. Randomly tie marbles into the second piece with embroidery thread. Mix the blue dye in 1 pint of boiling water in a heat-proof jug and add 1 tablespoon vinegar to the solution (but check the manufacturer's instructions). Because silk does not react well to boiling water, allow it to cool to 120°F before pouring the dye into the bowl. Place the tightly bound bundle of silk in the blue dye.

2 Mix the yellow dye in the same way and place it in the fabric with the marbles tied into it. Leave both pieces for about 20 minutes. Do not throw away the blue dye because you will need it again. Remove each bundle and rinse thoroughly under the cold tap until the water runs clear. Untie each bundle and allow the silk to dry flat. You can iron damp silk with a medium hot iron, and you may wish to speed up the drying process in this way.

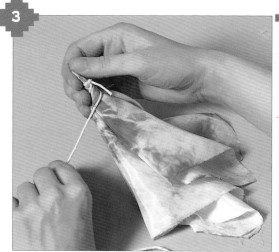

3 When the blue square is dry, find the center and pinch it so that the fabric falls into folds like a closed umbrella. Cross-bind it down three-quarters of its length, starting at the pinched center.

4 Fold the yellow square diagonally twice so that it forms a triangle and pleat it along its length, ironing the folds at each turn. Bind it with five pieces of twine along its length.

5 Mix the red dye, allow it to cool and place the blue square in the red dye. Place the yellow square in the blue dye. Leave both pieces for at least 20 minutes. Rinse each piece thoroughly in cold running water. Untie, allow to dry completely and iron.

6 Use à viewing window or two L-shaped pieces of card to select areas to cut and mount for your cards and gift tags.

7 We used a round wooden brooch blank and a semicircular metal blank and oval earring drops, which you can obtain from most good craft shops and some department stores. If you use adhesive to hold the fabric in place, take care not to get it on the front of the silk, which will be spoiled.

8 Button blanks usually have removable backs. Make sure that you keep the fabric taut and even over the front while you clip in the back sections.

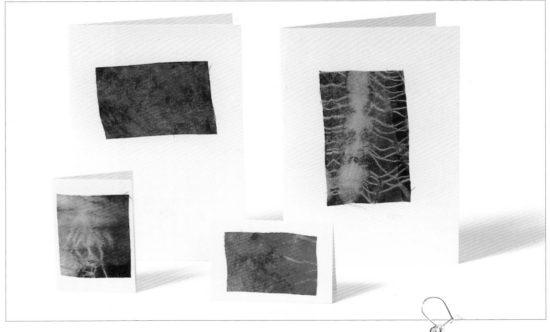

SOCKS AND HAIR SCRUNCHIES

The basic principles of tie-dyeing apply no matter what object you choose to decorate, whether it is plain fabric or a ready-made item. When you are selecting a method, however, you should consider the construction of the piece you are planning to make, because some patterns are more effective on a larger scale. In addition, some fabrics, such as cotton jersey and non-woven materials, stretch when they are wet, so you may want to bear this in mind when you plan your design.

You will need

◇ 1 pair of white, plain flat-weave, cotton socks
◇ 3 pieces of fabric, each 39 x 1 inches
◇ 2 hair scrunchies (see opposite)
◇ 39 inches string
◇ ¼ teaspoon each of orange, light green and violet dye
◇ 1 teaspoon salt
◇ 2 teaspoons vinegar (but check manufacturer's instructions)

TIP

• When you buy articles such as socks to tie-dye, avoid those made of ribbed cotton jersey, which tends to stretch out of shape when it is immersed in water. A small amount of nylon – not more than 10 per cent – will help to prevent the socks from twisting and bagging.

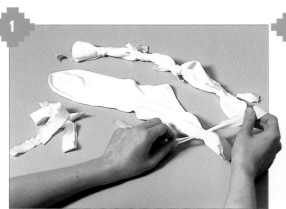

1 Cut one of the strips of fabric into eight pieces and tie four pieces at intervals around each sock.

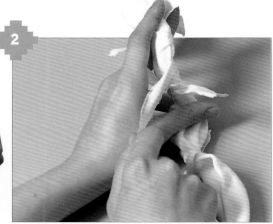

2 Use the remaining two strips to cross-bind each sock tightly along its length.

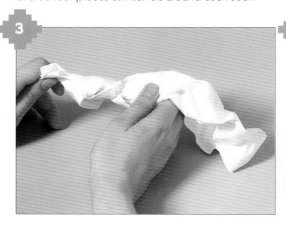

3 Tie three knots along the length of the first hair scrunchy.

4 Cross-bind the second scrunchy with string along its length.

5

6

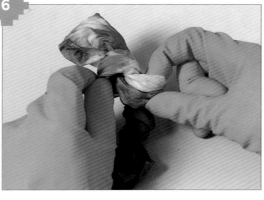

5 Mix the dyes, adding 1 teaspoon salt to the orange dye and 1 teaspoon of vinegar to the others. You will need about 1 pint of each color. Place the socks in one color and a scrunchy in each of the other colors. Leave them for about 20 minutes.

6 Remove the items from the dyes, rinse thoroughly and allow to dry. If the socks have stretched slightly, try drying them in a tumble dryer to shrink them back into shape.

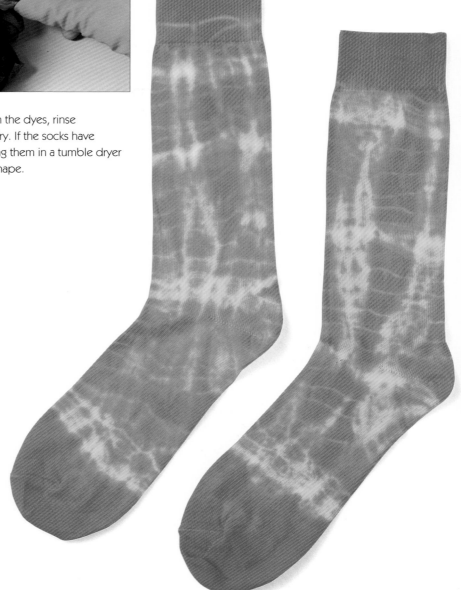

MAKING 2 HAIR SCRUNCHIES

You will need
◊ 2 pieces medium weight habutai silk, each 28 x 4 inches
◊ Needle and sewing cotton
◊ 4 inches fine string
◊ 14 inches fine elastic
◊ Bodkin or safety pin

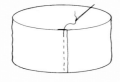
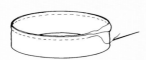

- With right sides together, stitch the two short ends of one piece of silk together to form a circle, then fold the fabric in half lengthways.
- Still with right sides together, stitch along the long edge to form a tube, leaving a small opening. Turn the silk back to the right side and repeat the process with the second piece of silk. Dye the scrunchies as described above.

- When they are dry, tie a piece of fine string to the elastic and use a bodkin or safety pin to thread it through the opening in the tube.
- Untie the string, pull up the elastic and tie the ends together, over-sewing them for extra security if you wish. Neatly oversew the opening. Alternatively, use two ready-made, plain scrunchies.

COLORED T-SHIRT

We have chosen to dye a plain colored T-shirt a deeper shade of its original color, and this allows us to develop a range of hues of one main color. You might prefer to experiment with the other primary colors – red and yellow – but unless you are especially fond of earthy colors, it would be as well to avoid over-dyeing material that is already dyed in a secondary color – orange, green or purple – with its opposite in the color spectrum (see the color wheel on page 21).

You will need
◇ 1 bright blue cotton T-shirt
◇ 1 large and 2 small marbles
◇ 6 feet string
◇ 1 bowl, large enough to hold 3 pints
◇ 1½ teaspoons navy blue dye
◇ 1 teaspoon salt

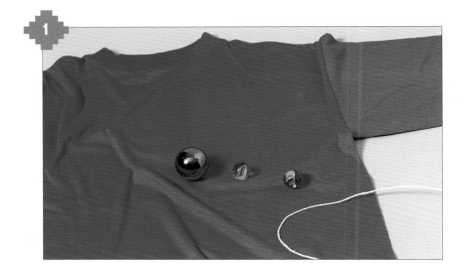

1 If you are using a new T-shirt, wash it in cool water and leave it to dry. This will remove any dressing on the fabric that might resist the dye.

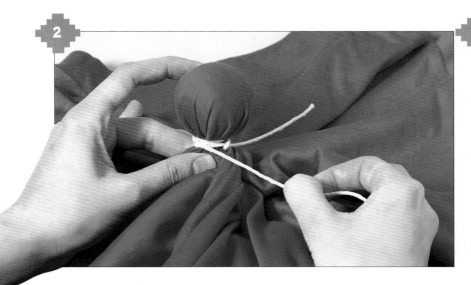

2 So that the pattern appears on the front only, separate the front from the back and use string to bind the large marble into the center of the front.

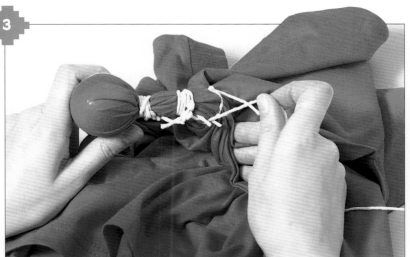

3 Wind the string around several times, leave a gap and then bind the fabric twice more to make a concentric pattern.

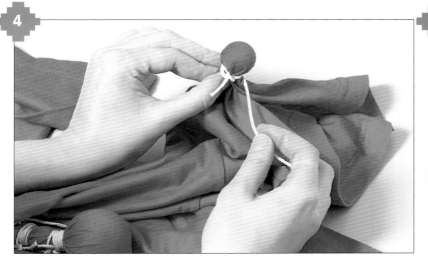

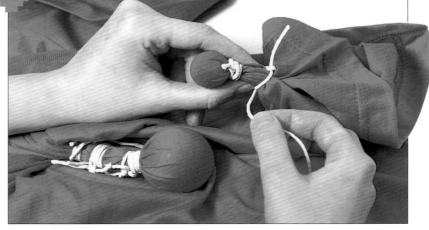

4 Bind a small marble into the shoulder fold of a sleeve, leave a gap and bind again.

5 Repeat on the other shoulder.

6 Mix the dye according to the manufacturer's instructions and add the salt. Allow the dye to cool. If the T-shirt is not made from good quality jersey, you may prefer to leave the dye until it is cold, which will help to overcome the problem of stretching. Place the T-shirt in the bowl.

7 Leave the T-shirt in the dye for about 20 minutes, stirring it frequently to prevent streaks being created and then rinse the T-shirt until the water runs clear.

8 Untie the string keeping the T-shirt over the bowl to prevent dripping. If it has stretched slightly, you may want to dry the T-shirt in a tumble-dryer to shrink it a little, and ironing will also help get it back into shape if necessary.

SILK SCARF

There are many different kinds of silk, and these vary greatly in price. You should, however, be able to buy a suitable length of lightweight habutai or pongee silk relatively inexpensively. Alternatively, you may prefer to personalize a scarf that you already own. We have used three different colours and two tying methods to produce a subtle, delicately shaded pattern.

You will need

◇ 36 x 36 inches undyed, lightweight habutai silk
◇ Electric iron
◇ 13 feet twine
◇ 6 feet 6 inches heavy thread or 2-ply wool
◇ 1 teaspoon each of deep rose, golden yellow and marine blue dye
◇ 6 tablespoons vinegar (but check manufacturer's instructions)
◇ 1 bowl, large enough to hold at least 2 pints

TIP
• If you choose to dye a scarf that is already colored, remember that the original color of the fabric will affect the result. A blue scarf dyed with yellow will, for example, become green (see the color wheel on page 21).

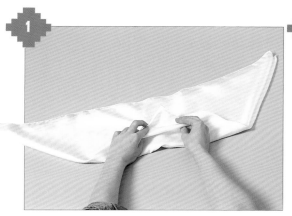

1 Before binding your scarf, iron it to remove any creases; you may find it easier to iron silk that is slightly damp. Fold the silk square diagonally to form a triangle, then fold it in half again to make a smaller triangle.

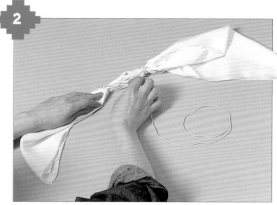

2 Pleat the silk lengthways and bind the folded strip with pieces of twine, placed at intervals of about 2½ inches, and fasten securely. Mid-way between each piece of twine, tie lengths of heavy thread tightly around the silk.

3 Mix 1 teaspoon deep rose dye in 2 pints of hot water and allow it to cool to 120°F. If the kind of dye you are using requires the addition of vinegar when silk is dyed, add 2 tablespoons to the solution. Place the pleated and bound silk scarf into the dye bath, making sure that the bowl is large enough to allow the material to move freely and that the dye solution is sufficiently deep to cover the material completely to make sure that it is evenly colored.

TIP
• If you are using dye colors that are either very strong or very dilute, you may wish to alter the dye to water ratios. In general, the final color is determined both by the concentration of the dye and by the length of time that the object is immersed in the dye.

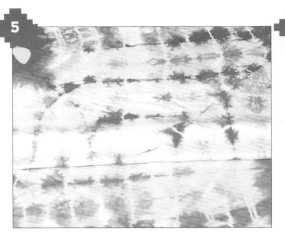

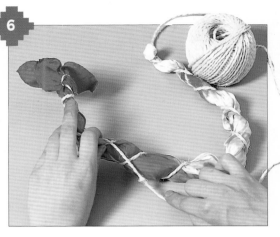

4 Leave the scarf in the bowl for at least 15 minutes, stirring it occasionally. When you have achieved the shade you want, remove the dye from the bowl and rinse the scarf under cold running water until the water runs clear. Then untie the twine and thread.

5 Allow the silk to dry flat. You may iron it when it is still slightly damp to remove all creases. Find the center of the square, pinch it and allow the silk to fall into drapes as if it were a closed umbrella.

6 Cross-bind the silk tightly with twine from top to bottom, mix the yellow dye and proceed as before.

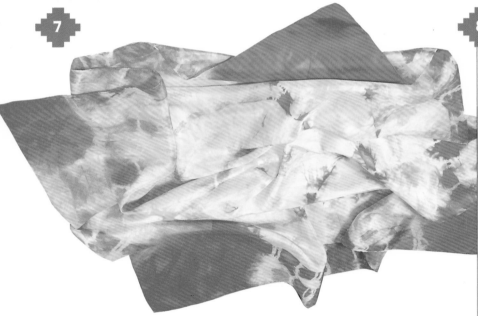

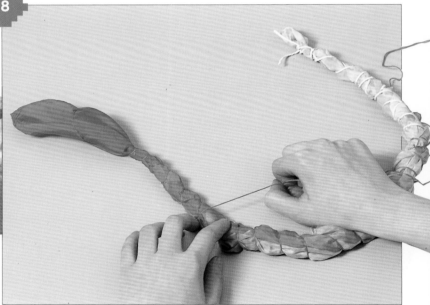

7 Rinse thoroughly, untie and dry before ironing to remove the creases.

8 Pinch and fold the silk as in step 5 and use twine to bind the top half. Bind the bottom half of the scarf more tightly with heavy thread so that more blue dye can reach the center of the scarf. Mix the blue dye as before and place the bound scarf in the bowl. You may wish to dilute the blue dye, because marine blue can be rather strong and may over-power the deep rose and yellow pattern.

9

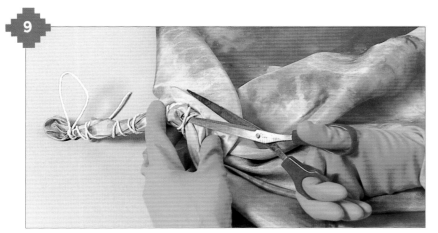

$\mathcal{9}$ Rinse the silk thoroughly before untying the scarf and allow it to dry.

COLOR WHEEL

• Dyes behave differently from pigment-based colors – paints and inks, for example – because they rely on some form of chemical agent such as salt or vinegar to make them permanent. This attribute makes it difficult to judge accurately what the end result will be, and tie-dyeing colored fabric or an already dyed item of clothing can add to this unpredictability. In general, however, you should be able to anticipate more or less what the end result will be, and you can use this wheel as a guide.

CUSHION COVERS

As you experiment with different kinds of fabric you will notice that different materials accept dyes in different ways. When they are bound and dyed, cotton and thicker fabrics, especially cotton lawn and cotton poplin, take on a softer, almost dusty pattern, which tends to be stronger on one side. This quality makes them acceptable for use in soft furnishings, where only one side of the fabric is visible. We have made two square cushion covers, which are easy to make and yet can bring an individual and highly personal accent to your home. The materials listed here are sufficient to make two double-sided cushion covers, each measuring 18 x 18 inches.

You will need
◇ 4 pieces of fabric, each 26 x 26 inches
◇ Electric iron
◇ 13 feet twine
◇ 1 packet of dye in each of golden yellow, marine blue and copper (or colors to suit your furnishing scheme)
◇ 1 bowl, large enough to hold 3 pints
◇ 2 cushion pads, each 18 x 18 inches

TIP

• Some colored twines – those that are sold for garden use, for example – may stain fabrics when they are dampened by the dye solution. Wooden clothes pegs may also retain traces of dye, and if you re-use them you may find that minute quantities of the original color are transferred to your new pattern. These colors may enhance your design or they may ruin it – so take care.

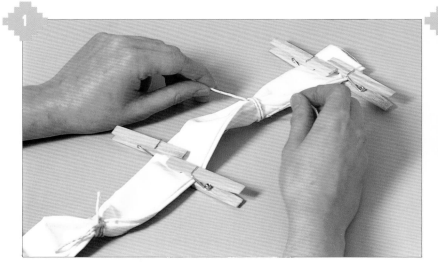

1 Iron the squares of material to remove any creases, and for the first cover, fold the material in half then pleat it lengthways, making the pleats about 1¼ inches wide. Iron again. Secure the pleats with clothes pegs, spacing the pegs at intervals of about 2½ inches. Bind the fabric with twine between each peg.

2 For the second cover, pinch the material in the center and allow it to fall into drapes. Twist the fabric slightly, then tightly cross-bind it along its entire length with twine to limit the amount of dye that comes into contact with the material. This technique is especially useful for adding small splashes of color.

MAKING A CUSHION

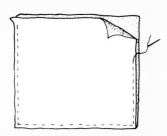

- Place two matching squares together, right sides facing, and stitch around three sides, leaving a seam allowance of about 3cm (1¼in), although the seam may vary if your material has shrunk slightly during the dyeing process.

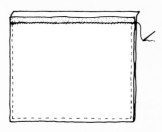

- Fold down and iron a 2.5cm (1in) hem along both edges.

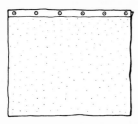

- Add a zip fastener, Velcro or press-studs to close the opening before turning to the right side and inserting the cushion pad.

TIP

- If you are making larger cushion covers, remember to increase the amounts of water and dye you mix and to use a large bowl so that the pieces of material can be completely submerged.

3 Mix the yellow dye, making sure that you use a bowl that is large enough to accommodate all the pieces of fabric. Add the salt to the dye bath if recommended by the manufacturer. Place both covers in the yellow dye and leave for 15–20 minutes, stirring occasionally. Remove the covers, rinse thoroughly and untie.

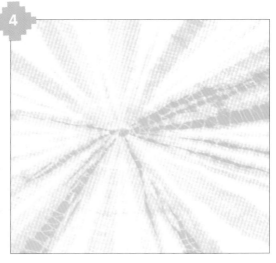

4 Dry the fabric and iron it. If the fabric is very creased, you may find it easier to use the steam setting on your iron or to dampen the material slightly to make ironing easier.

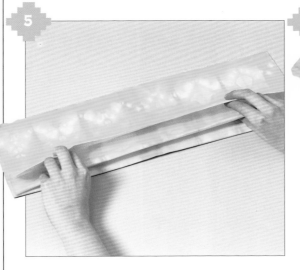

5 Take the first square and fold it in half, across the dyed lines then pleat it.

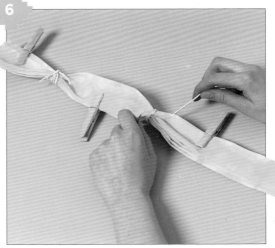

6 Iron and pleat the square, securing it with pegs and twine as before. Mix the blue dye and place the folded and tied material in it. Leave for 15–20 minutes, rinse thoroughly, untie and dry.

7

7 Take the second, ironed cover and pinch it in the center to drape it in an umbrella shape. Cross-bind it half-way down its length with twine. Mix the copper dye and place the tied material in it. Leave for 15–20 minutes, rinse thoroughly, untie and dry.

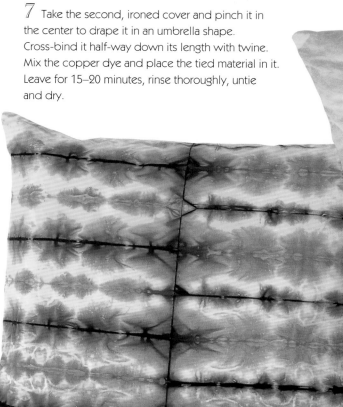

LEGGINGS

Predicting how a pattern will turn out on a ready-made item of clothing is difficult because of such variable factors as the cut of the item and the weight and type of fabric that has been used. Most items of leisure-wear now contain a small percentage of lycra, which helps to keep them in shape but which, unfortunately, does not dye easily. The amount of lycra in the article may, therefore, result in the final color being lighter than you had expected. We have chosen to dye a pair of cotton leggings.

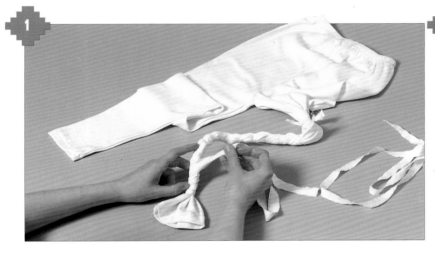

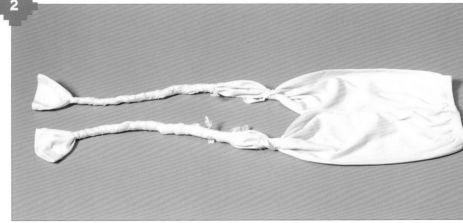

You will need
◇ 1 pair ecru leggings
◇ 2 strips of fabric, each 10 x 1 inches
◇ 4 strips of fabric, each 5 feet x 1 inch
◇ 1½ teaspoons each of black and old gold dye
◇ 2 teaspoons salt
◇ 1 bowl, large enough to hold 3 pints

TIP

• You may find that black dye does not produce jet black. This is because intense, deep black is an incredibly difficult color to achieve. Try adding a little more black dye to the dye bath to create a darker shade. The shade will also depend on the quality of dye you are using – more expensive dyes tend to produce truer colors.

1 Take the cotton leggings and bind each leg 3 inches down from the gusset with short strips of fabric. Dyeing some tied items can lead to patterns appearing in inappropriate places, so some areas, such as the gusset and seat, should be left plain.

2 Leave a space of about 3 inches, then cross-bind down each length of 2 inches from the foot. You will need two strips for each leg.

3 Mix the old gold dye in 3 pints of hot water and add 1 tablespoon of salt or mix according to the manufacturer's instructions. Allow the water to cool before adding the leggings so that the garment does not stretch. Leave the leggings in the bowl for at least 20 minutes, remove and rinse thoroughly. When the water runs clear, wring the leggings out so that they no longer drip.

4 Mix the black dye as above or according to the manufacturer's instructions and place the top half of the leggings – that is, the unbound section – into the bowl, leaving the bound legs hanging over the edge of the bowl. Stand the bowl on plenty of old newspapers in case the leggings continue to drip dilute dye. Leave the leggings in the dye for at least 20 minutes.

5 Rinse thoroughly in cold water before untying the legs. Because the fabric was still wet from the previous dyeing, the black dye will have crept along the legs to give a mottled, vignetted effect.

ALL-IN-ONE COTTON BODY

◆

Combining several techniques in one item of clothing can produce fairly spectacular results. Although the final pattern can look complicated, the tie-dying process means that decorating in this way is relatively straightforward. Here, we have dyed a white all-in-one cotton body by using two colors and two different techniques to produce a three-color pattern. This project also demonstrates how easy it is to isolate a pattern and color on the same article.

You will need
◇ 1 white all-in-one cotton body
◇ 1 large marble or glass ball
◇ 24 inches string
◇ 4 strips of fabric, each 5 feet x 1 inch
◇ 1½ teaspoons each of bright pink and violet dye
◇ 1 bowl, large enough to hold 6 pints
◇ 2 tablespoons salt

1 Bind the large marble into the chest of the cotton body, making sure that you bind the string from the front of the garment, which will give slightly different circular patterns on the back and the front. Take each arm, twist it slightly and then tightly cross-bind each one with strips of fabric. You will need two strips for each arm. Twisting the fabric before binding stops the dye from saturating the whole of the sleeve.

2 Mix the pink dye in 1 pint of boiling water. Add the solution to a bowl containing 5 pints of warm water. Add the salt and allow to cool. Dye the whole garment, stirring it to help prevent patchy coloring and leaving it for a further 20–30 minutes. The longer you leave it, the brighter the color will be. Rinse thoroughly in cold running water.

TIP
• Remember that the poorer the quality of the article you are dyeing, the cooler the dye solution should be before you place the item in it.

3 Wring the excess water from the garment and mix the violet dye. Place the gusset end of the body, up to the waist, and the bottom half of the sleeves into the dye. Leave for a further 20–30 minutes.

4 Remove from the dye, rinse thoroughly and untie. Tumble dry and iron to remove creases and any stretching that may have occurred.

SILK BOXER SHORTS

The softness and sheen of some types of silk make them ideal for underclothes, and the finish on silk also affects the way that the dyes take on the fabric. Dyeing flat woven or satin silk with acid tones, such as citrus yellow, fire red, bright green or hot orange, produces some dramatic results. We have used a pair of habutai silk boxer shorts for this project, dyeing them with citrus yellow and bright green to give a vibrant patterned effect.

You will need
◇ 1 pair white habutai silk boxer shorts
◇ 15–20 elastic bands
◇ ½ teaspoon each of citrus yellow and bright green dye
◇ 4 tablespoons vinegar (but check manufacturer's instructions)
◇ 1 bowl, large enough to hold 3 pints

1 Lay the boxer shorts on your work surface and separate the front from the back. Randomly bunch small areas of both back and front and bind them with elastic bands.

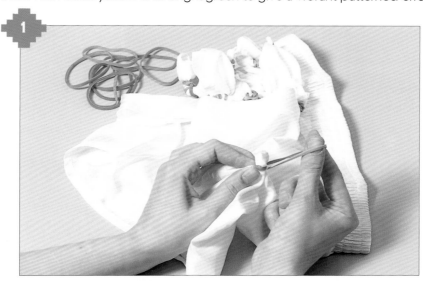

2 Mix the yellow dye in 1 pint of boiling water and add 2 tablespoons of vinegar. Add the solution to a bowl containing a further 2 pints of hot water and allow it to cool to 120°F before adding the shorts. Leave the shorts for 20–30 minutes, stirring occasionally.

3 Remove the shorts from the dye, rinse thoroughly, remove the elastic bands and allow to dry.

5

6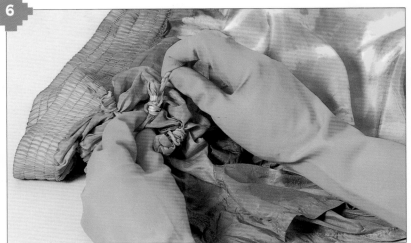

4 Repeat steps 1 and 2, but with the green dye. After 20–30 minutes, remove the shorts and rinse thoroughly.

5 When the water runs clear, remove the elastic bands and leave the shorts to dry flat.

SILK SARONG

The ruche method of tying makes it possible to create wonderfully vignetted patterns, which gradually fade along the length of the material. Using two or more colors allows you to build up multicolored designs, in which bold motifs merge into subtler patterns. We have used a simple binding technique with a contrasting color to decorate a simple cotton top and briefs to create an ideal compliment to the silk sarong for those hot sunny days on the beach.

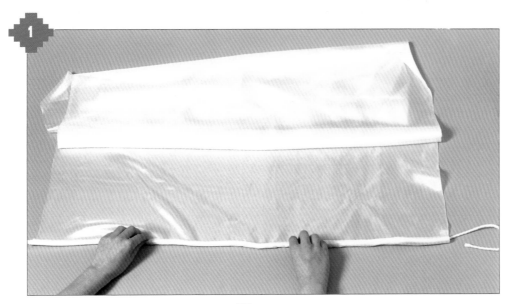

You will need
- ◇ 1 piece lightweight habutai or pongee silk, 6 x 3 feet
- ◇ Electric iron
- ◇ 3 feet 3 inches thick cord (plastic washing line, for example)
- ◇ 1 large marble and 2 medium sized marbles
- ◇ 6 feet string
- ◇ 1 teaspoon each of bright red, bright blue and bright green dye
- ◇ 6 tablespoons vinegar (but check manufacturer's instructions)
- ◇ 1 bowl, large enough to hold at least 4 pints
- ◇ Top and briefs in 100 per cent white cotton
- ◇ 2 lengths of thick twine or string, each about 3 feet 3 inches
- ◇ 2 tablespoons salt

1 Iron the silk to remove the creases and lay it on your work surface with a short side towards you. Place the cord across the end nearest to you and roll the fabric around the cord until about 12 inches remains unrolled.

2 Holding one end of the roll, push the fabric at the other end down the cord as far as it will go. Tie the ends of the cord tightly together with a double knot so that you have a circle of tightly ruched material with a flap.

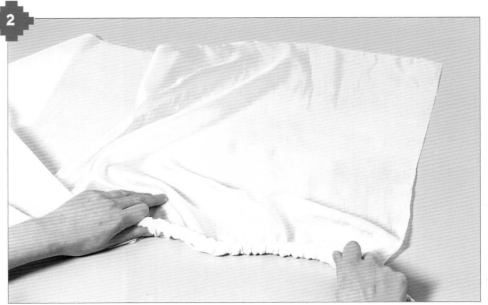

3

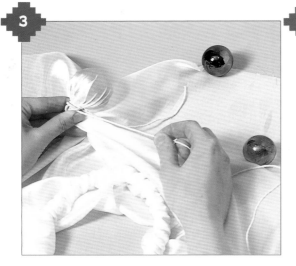

3 Use string to bind the large marble in the center of this trailing piece of material. Bind the two smaller marbles at either side of the large marble.

4

4 Mix the blue dye in 2 pints boiling water, add 3 tablespoons of vinegar and add the solution to a bowl containing a further 2 pints of hot water. Allow to cool to 120°F before adding the silk. Leave for 30 minutes. Remove the fabric from the dye, rinse thoroughly and untie. Leave the silk to dry and iron it.

5

5 Place the silk on your work surface with the section in which the marbles were tied nearest to you. Repeat steps 1–4, but use the red dye.

6

6 Rinse and untie the silk, then iron dry.

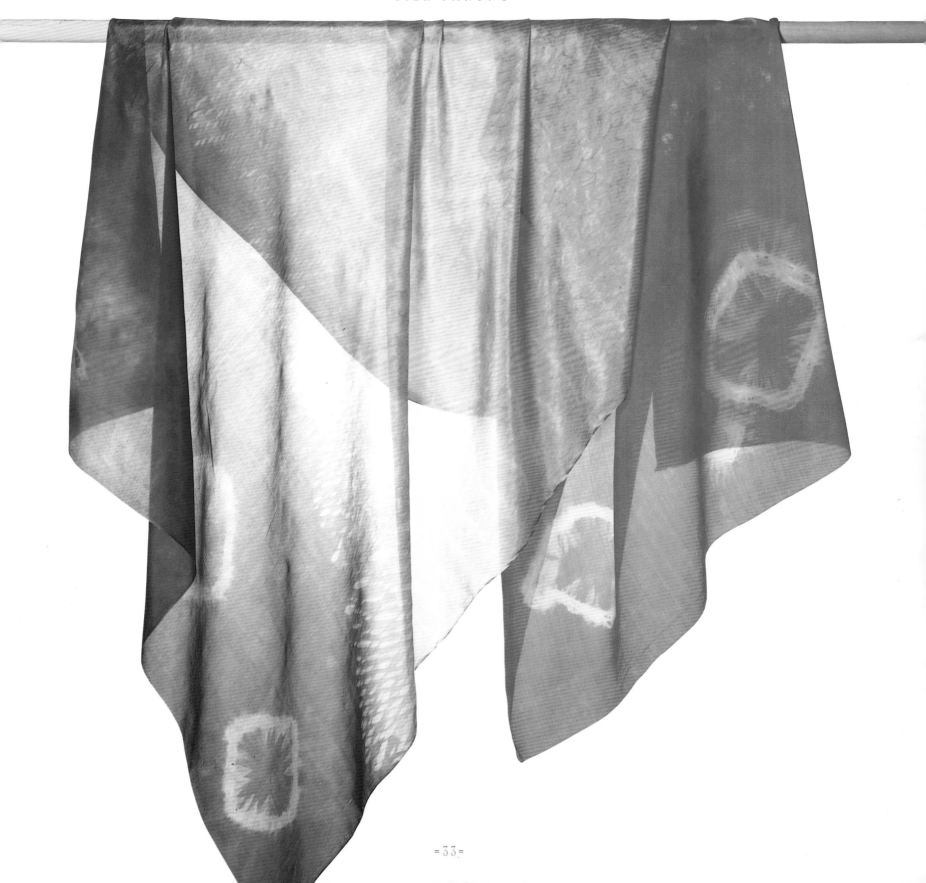

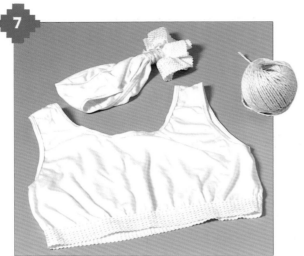

7 While the silk is dyeing you can prepare the cotton top and briefs for dyeing.

8 Use the two lengths of thick twine to bind around the width of the briefs just below the waistband and across the top of the chest. Mix the green dye in 2 pints of boiling water and add the salt. Add this solution to a bowl containing a further 2 pints of hot water. Allow to cool before adding the top and briefs. Leave them for 20–30 minutes before rinsing thoroughly, untying and drying.

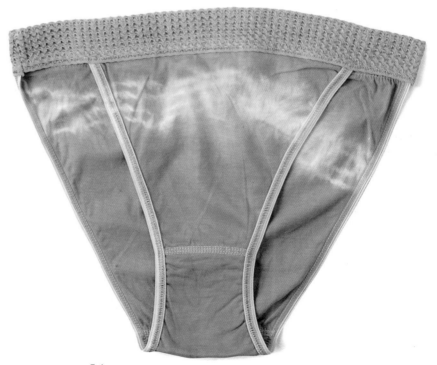

Long-sleeved Ecru Cotton Top with Appliqué Motif

◆

Mixing and matching different kinds of fabric within one project is an effective way of adding spots of color and texture to a design or item of clothing. For this project we have chosen to pattern a long-sleeved ecru cotton top in a single color and then appliqué a small piece of multicolored silk to the chest. Back the silk with medium weight cotton to stop it from twisting.

You will need

◇ 1 long-sleeved cotton top
◇ 10 feet string
◇ 2 teaspoons black dye
◇ 2 tablespoons salt
◇ 1 bowl, large enough to hold at least 6 pints
◇ 1 piece of medium weight habutai silk, 12 x 12 inches
◇ Electric iron
◇ 10 elastic bands
◇ ⅛ teaspoon each of navy blue and orange dye
◇ 4 tablespoons vinegar (but check manufacturer's instructions)
◇ 1 bowl, large enough to hold at least 2 pints
◇ 24 inches heavy thread
◇ 1 piece of fine ecru cotton lawn, 5 x 5 inches

1 Lay the top on your work surface with the neck furthest away from you. Take a side of the body in each hand and pleat the sides towards the centre.

2 Use 5 feet of string to cross-bind the body from 10 inches down from the neck to the bottom hem.

3 Take each arm and cross-bind them separately, pleating them as you did the body and binding from 1 inch up from the wrist to the shoulder seam.

4

5

4 Mix the black dye and salt in 2 pints of boiling water and add it to a bowl containing 4 pints of hot water. You may want to test the strength of the dye by dipping a strip of cotton into the bowl for about 10 minutes. To obtain a really dense black you may need to add more dye.

5 Allow the solution to cool so that the fabric does not stretch and add the top, stirring occasionally to encourage the dye to spread evenly. The longer you leave the garment in the dye, the darker the shade of black that will be produced.

6 When the top is as dark as possible, which may take 45 minutes, remove it from the dye, rinse thoroughly and untie. You may want to put it through the tumble dryer if it has stretched slightly.

6

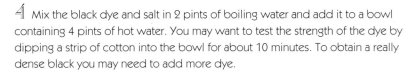

TIP
• When you are appliquéing fabric that is different from the garment or base material, remember that they may shrink at different rates, so if you are unsure, wash, dry and iron both pieces separately before you begin.

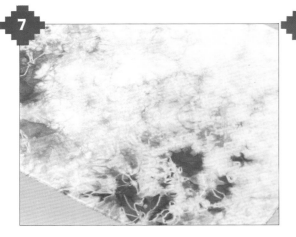

7 While the shirt is drying, dye the silk. Scrunch it into a tight ball and bind it with embroidery thread. Mix the blue dye in boiling water and add 1 tablespoon vinegar. Allow the dye to cool to 120°F before adding the silk, which should be left for 15–20 minutes. Remove the silk from the blue dye, rinse thoroughly and untie.

8 Dry the silk, ironing it with a medium hot iron to speed the process, fold it in half, twist it and allow it to fold back on itself.

9 Cross-bind it tightly with heavy thread. Mix the orange dye as in step 8 and add the silk. Leave the silk for 15–20 minutes before rinsing thoroughly, untying and ironing. Take the piece of cotton lawn and turn under and iron a hem of about ½ inch all round.

MAKING THE PATCH

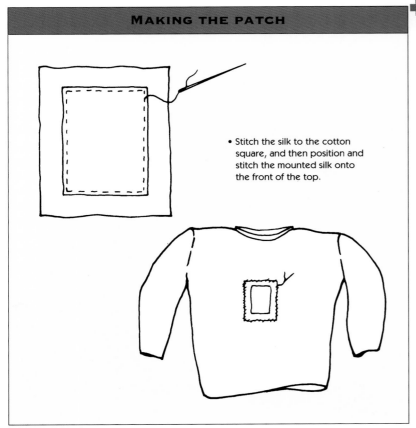

• Stitch the silk to the cotton square, and then position and stitch the mounted silk onto the front of the top.

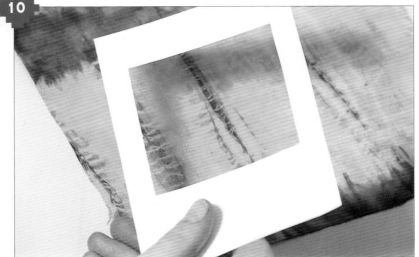

10 Use a viewing window or two L-shaped sections to select and cut out a 4 x 4 inch section of the patterned silk.

SHORT-SLEEVED SILK TOP

Silk is a wonderfully versatile fabric, and there are dozens of ways in which it can be woven to produce different types of material, each with its own qualities and properties. Silk can be more robust than cotton, especially knitted materials such as cotton jersey, which can easily stretch out of shape. This project involves dyeing a silk *crêpe de chine* top. The material is slightly stretchy, but it takes dye well and gives a rich, lustrous finish. To build up texture, we initially bind and dye the silk with a light color, and although this shade will not be obvious when the other color is added, it provides subtle variations of tone that become visible in certain lights.

You will need
◇ 1 *crêpe de chine* short-sleeved top
◇ 5 corks
◇ 6 feet 6 inches heavy thread
◇ 2 tablespoons each of citrus yellow and bright red dye
◇ 8 tablespoons vinegar (but check manufacturer's instructions)
◇ 1 bowl, large enough to hold at least 6 pints
◇ 36 inches thick cord (nylon washing line is best)

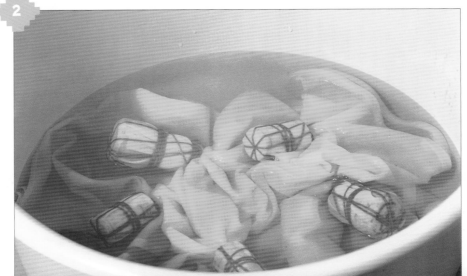

1 Randomly bind all the corks into the top. If you prefer, use other objects such as egg-cups or buttons.

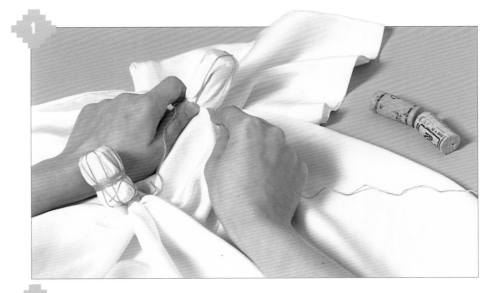

2 Mix the citrus yellow dye in 2 pints of boiling water and add 4 tablespoons of vinegar. Add this to a basin containing a further 4 pints of hot water. Allow the dye to cool to 120°F before adding the silk. Leave in the dye for 30 minutes, stirring occasionally.

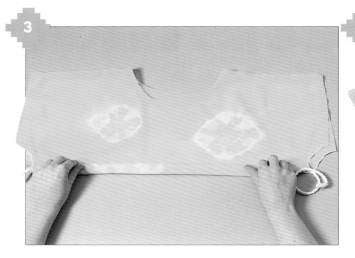

3 Once the silk has dyed, remove it, rinse it thoroughly and untie it. Dry the silk, ironing it to remove any creases. Place the top on your work surface with the neck away from you, and roll the garment around the thick cord, leaving about 10 inches at the top unrolled.

4 Hold one end of the rolled material and ruche the top along the cord as far as you can. Tie the two ends of the cord together firmly in a double knot.

5 Mix the bright red dye in 2 pints of boiling water and add 4 tablespoons of vinegar. Add this to a further 4 pints of hot water. Allow the dye to cool to 120°F before adding the ruched silk. Leave in the dye for 30 minutes, stirring occasionally. Remove the material, untie and dry flat.

SOFA THROW

So far we have dyed silk and cotton fabric or ready-made items, but most cold water dyes will also take well on wool, linen, rayon or viscose. A sofa throw needs to be fairly heavy, and this project uses wool lawn, which is sometimes known as nun's veiling. When you are dyeing wool, remember that it tends to stretch when it is wet and that new or virgin wool will still contain lanolin, the sheep's own waterproofing. You can either try to remove most of the lanolin by washing the wool before you begin or you can do as we have done here, which is to dye the wool straight from the roll, which adds a degree of unpredictability to the end result.

You will need
- ◇ 3 feet 3 inches x 3 feet 3 inches wool lawn (if the measure is narrow, you may need 2 lengths, stitched together)
- ◇ 10 feet heavy string
- ◇ 2 teaspoons copper dye
- ◇ 10 tablespoons vinegar (but check manufacturer's instructions)
- ◇ 1 bowl, large enough to hold at least 6 pints
- ◇ 1 teaspoon black dye
- ◇ 1 bowl, large enough to hold at least 4 pints

1 Pinch the fabric in the center and allow it to fall in drapes like a closed umbrella. If you are using a rectangle the fabric will not fall evenly, but this will not affect the end result. Working from the center of the fabric, cross-bind it with heavy string to about 12 inches from the bottom. At 3 inch intervals bind around the shape several times.

2 Mix the copper dye in 2 pints of boiling water and add 6 tablespoons of vinegar. Add the solution to a bowl containing a further 4 pints of hot water. Allow the dye to cool to 120°F, then add the bound wool. If you have not pre-washed the wool you will find that the dye will take several minutes to penetrate the surface fibers.

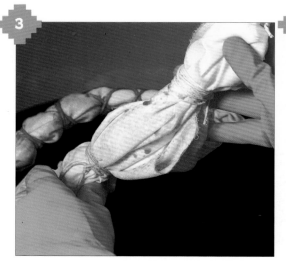

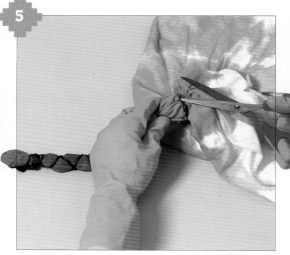

3 Encourage the dyeing process by stirring the dye bath. Leave the wool in the dye for 30–45 minutes. If you have not pre-washed the wool, the shade will be several shades lighter than if you have, and for this reason the dye described here is fairly concentrated.

4 While the wool is in the copper dye, mix the black dye in 2 pints of boiling water and add 4 tablespoons of vinegar. Add this mixture to a further 2 pints of hot water. Allow this to cool. Remove the fabric from the copper dye, then place the tip of the bundle, the center of the fabric, into the black dye, draping the rest of the fabric over the side of the bowl. Immerse about 8 inches of the bundle in the black dye and leave for a further 40 minutes. Not rinsing out the copper dye before adding the black allows the wool to continue to absorb the copper dye. This stage can be messy, so if you cannot stand the bowl on a draining board, make sure that your work surface is covered with plenty of newspaper to absorb the drips.

5 After 40 minutes rinse the wool in cold running water and then untie. Do not wring out the wool, which will probably stretch it out of shape.

6 The naturally occurring lanolin will have acted as a kind of resist, and when you spread out the wool you will find small, irregular patches that have remained undyed.

SILK GEORGETTE SHIRT

◆

Different weights of fabric accept dyes in different ways. When they are tie-dyed, lighter weight materials
and loosely woven fabrics tend to yield softer patterns, and it is worth considering the weight and
density of the weave before you decide on your tying methods. For example, sharp, pleated
designs are most effective on tightly woven, flat fabrics. Silk georgette, on the other hand, is a soft,
open-weave silk, rather similar to chiffon or silk muslin, and you could use either of these materials
or cotton cheesecloth or cotton muslin instead.

You will need
◇ 1 silk georgette shirt, either ready-made or one you
   have made yourself
◇ 10 feet string
◇ 1 teaspoon each of dusky rose and dark gray dye
◇ 4 tablespoons vinegar (but check manufacturer's
   instructions and if you are using cotton remember
   to use salt instead)
◇ 1 bowl, large enough to hold at least 3 pints

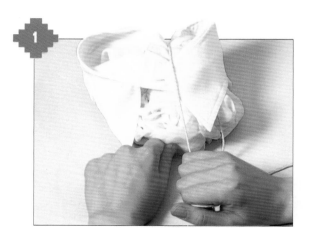

1 Bunch the shirt into a ball. Do not roll it, because
this will limit the area exposed to the dye. Secure
the bundle by wrapping string tightly around it. Mix
the dusky rose dye in 2 pints of boiling water. Add
2 tablespoons of vinegar (salt if you are dyeing
cotton) and add the mixture to a further 1 pint of
hot water. Allow the solution to cool to 120°F
before adding the shirt. Leave in the dye for
20–30 minutes.

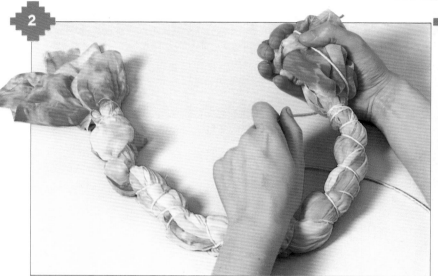

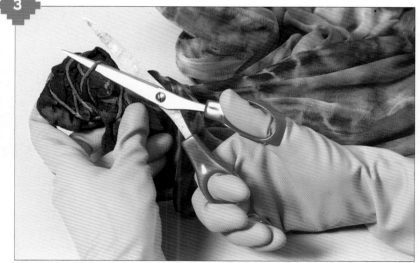

2 Remove the bundle from the dye, rinse thoroughly and untie. Dry the shirt flat
to help avoid creasing and shrinking. When the shirt is dry, bunch the collar and
neck into a ball and bind it with string. Loosely twist the body and sleeves
together, and cross-bind the entire length of the garment with string.

3 Mix the dark gray dye as in step 1 and, when the dye has cooled, add the
shirt to the bowl and leave it for a further 20–30 minutes. Remove the shirt from
the bowl, rinse thoroughly, untie the string and leave the shirt to dry flat.

TIP

• Many open-weave silk and cotton garments contain a dressing or stiffener, and you will get better results if you wash the article before you attempt to dye it.

DUVET COVER AND PILLOWCASES

<hr>

This duvet cover is built up in patterned panels, which are separated by plain panels of cotton lawn.
Constructing large pieces in this way overcomes the problems of color matching or under-dyeing
that can occur with large quantities of fabric.

You will need

◇ 4 pieces white cotton, each 6 feet 6 inches x 30 inches
◇ 2 pieces white cotton, each 26 x 20 inches
◇ Electric iron
◇ 52 clothes pegs
◇ 13 feet string
◇ 3 teaspoons dusky rose dye
◇ 1 teaspoon cornflower blue dye
◇ 4 tablespoons salt
◇ 1 bowl, large enough to hold at least 4 pints
◇ 2 pieces lightweight ecru cotton lawn, each 6 feet 6 inches x 30 inches
◇ 2 pieces lightweight ecru cotton lawn, each 26 x 20 inches

TIP

• Working with large amounts of fabric poses certain problems, especially when it comes to binding the material effectively and achieving an even color. When you are planning a project that requires a large amount of cloth you may find it easier to dye the fabric in panels and make the pieces into the item afterwards. Trying to color-match panels that have been dyed in separate dye baths is, unfortunately, one of the drawbacks of attempting to apply a pattern to a large item in this way. However, even if you were able to fit the whole piece of fabric in one dye bath, you would probably find that the color was unable to penetrate through to all areas of the fabric simply because of the mass of material.

ASSEMBLING THE DUVET

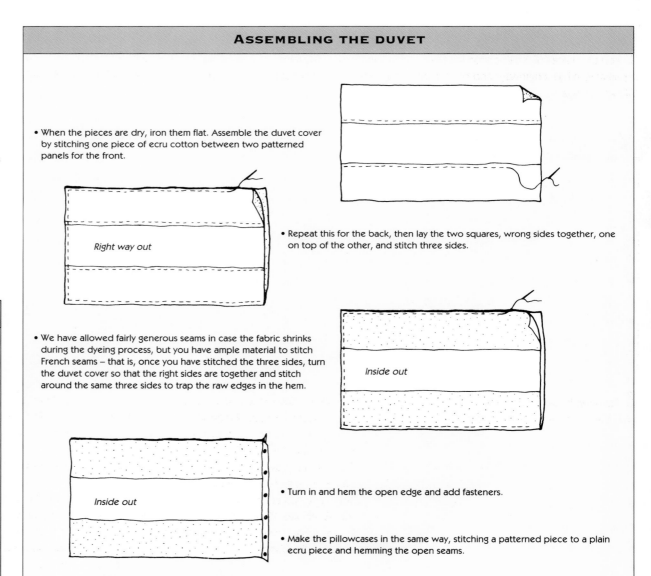

• When the pieces are dry, iron them flat. Assemble the duvet cover by stitching one piece of ecru cotton between two patterned panels for the front.

Right way out

• We have allowed fairly generous seams in case the fabric shrinks during the dyeing process, but you have ample material to stitch French seams – that is, once you have stitched the three sides, turn the duvet cover so that the right sides are together and stitch around the same three sides to trap the raw edges in the hem.

Inside out

• Repeat this for the back, then lay the two squares, wrong sides together, one on top of the other, and stitch three sides.

Inside out

• Turn in and hem the open edge and add fasteners.

• Make the pillowcases in the same way, stitching a patterned piece to a plain ecru piece and hemming the open seams.

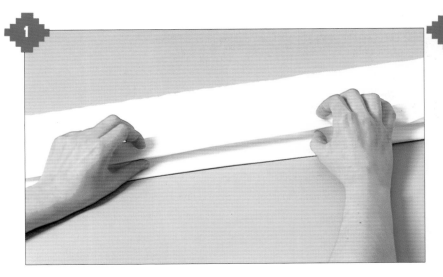

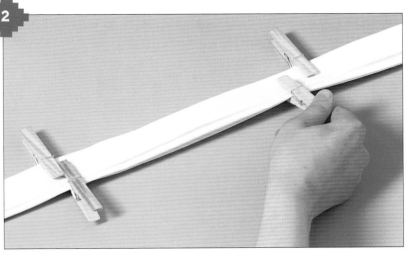

1 Iron the pieces of white cotton to remove any creases, then fold them, separately, in half lengthways and pleat them. Each pleat should be about 1¼ inches wide.

2 Iron the pleats and secure them with clothes pegs on both sides of the pleat, spacing the pegs at intervals of about 12 inches.

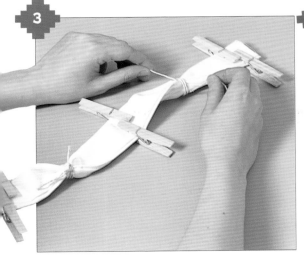

3 Half-way between each peg, bind the fabric with pieces of string about 9 inches long.

4 Mix the dusky rose dye in 2 pints of boiling water and add 2 tablespoons of salt. Add this solution to a further 12 pints of hot water. You must use a bowl that is large enough to hold the fabric and the dye comfortably. Place all the bound white fabric in the bowl while the dye is still hot if you want a particularly vibrant color. Leave it for 30–45 minutes. When the fabric is dyed, remove the bundles from the dye and rinse thoroughly but do not untie the bundles.

5 Mix the cornflower blue dye in 2 pints of boiling water and add the salt. Add this to a further 6 pints of hot water. Drape the pleated fabric over the bowl so that only the ends are in the dye – about 18 inches each end for the duvet cover and 8 inches each end for the pillowcases. Leave for a further 30 minutes. Remove the fabric from the dye, rinse thoroughly and untie the bundles. At this stage you can add an extra proprietary treatment to the fabric to make the dyes more permanent, but check the manufacturer's directions.